Everything I Don't Know

Everything I Don't Know

Selected Poems of Jerzy Ficowski

Translated from the Polish by
Jennifer Grotz and Piotr Sommer

Afterword by Piotr Sommer

WORLD POETRY BOOKS

World Poetry Books

Storrs, CT 06269

www.worldpoetrybooks.com

English translation copyright © 2021 by Jennifer Grotz and Piotr Sommer

Afterword copyright © 2021 by Piotr Sommer

This book is made possible with support from the Stavros Niarchos Foundation.

Library of Congress Cataloging-in-Publication Data

Names: Ficowski, Jerzy, author; Grotz, Jennifer and Sommer, Piotr, translators

Title: Everything I Don't Know / Jerzy Ficowski.

Description: Storrs, Connecticut : World Poetry Books [2021]

Identifiers: LCCN 2021940608

    ISBN 978-1-954218-99-4

Published in the United States of America

2 4 6 8 10 9 7 5 3 1

Cover photograph by Piotr Wójcik

Cover design by Kyle G. Hunter

Book design by Dakota Jackson

CONTENTS

My Sides of the World (1957)

Apricot Time   13
Behind the Door the World   14
O Drawer!   15
All Around London   16
Ante-Bird—Scarecrow   18

Amulets and Definitions (1960)

The Empty Places After   23
My Attempted Travels   25
The Migration of the Hangers   26
From the Mythological Encyclopedia   27
     i.   Burners   27
     ii.   Faucet   27
     iii. Ashtray   28
     iv. Table   28
     v.   Cone   29
     vi. Candle   29
Thursday   31
Inside-Out Views   32
Paris! Paris!   33
Entomology   34

Picture Alphabet (1962)

Picture Alphabet 37

Revolt 40

I Dreamt Myself 42

Fish on the Sand 43

Six Etudes 44

      i. Old Beggar at the Church 44

      ii. Cemetery Squirrels 44

      iii. Gordian Bow 45

      iv. Since Carp 46

      v. Erotic 46

      vi. All the Same 47

The Bird Beyond the Bird (1968)

Today a Long Time Ago 51

Life 52

Penetration 53

From Fingerprints 54

My Unsurvivor 55

Apocrypha of the Original Apple 57

Papusza 59

Creator 63

Traduction 64

Tell How It Was 66

The Bird Beyond the Bird 68

A Reading of Ashes (1979)

    *** (I was unable to save)   73

    The Assumption of Miriam

        from a Street in Winter, 1942   74

    5 VIII 1942   75

    The Six-Year Old from the Ghetto Begging

        on Smolna Street in the Year 1942   77

    The Jews Left   79

    The Execution of Memory   80

    A Gathering of Stones   82

    The End of the Rite   84

Illicit (1979)

    I'll Tell You a Story   87

    Illicit   89

    *** (With a temperature of 101.3)   90

    Gdańsk Train Station, Warsaw 1968   91

    The Hour Is Ripe   92

    Recipe   94

    The Rite   95

    How to Spoil the Cannibals' Fun   96

Errata (1981)

    Childhood, 1940   101

    A Certain Dickens   103

    Ringelblum Archive   104

Death of a Unicorn (1981)

Incantation 107

Getting Out of the Mirror 108

*** (in the steep evenings of falling asleep) 110

Don't Be Surprised 111

Tangolia, 1936 112

List of Telephone Subscribers for the Capital
    City of Warsaw for the Year 1938-39 114

There I'll Get Lost 116

Refuge 117

Slowness 118

*** (Honey lives only) 119

Prayer to the Holy Louse 121

The Gypsy Road 124

Village Landscape 126

The Initial (1994)

The Initial 129

Everything I Don't Know 130

The Road to Zuzela 132

From the Nature Notebook 133

My Belated Guests 137

Memorial 138

The Dot over the I 139

Freedom 140

Paired Inscription 141

Beforetime and Aftertime (2004)

Dear Zbigniew   145
Absent   146
I'm Heading Out   148
*** (rivers suspend their current)   149
Kazakhstan, USSR   150
from "Side Notes"   151

Pantarheia (2006)

By Itself   163
Aequinoctium   164
Wormwood Night   166
Pantarheia   168
Screening Cancelled   170
We   172

Afterword by Piotr Sommer   175

Biographical Notes   184
Acknowledgments   186

from *My Sides of the World*

1957

Apricot Time

It's probably right here
out of the ripe moon rising
that a pit fell once
(because it isn't just the moon's
other side we don't know
but also its pit!)
and that's what started
the apricot orchards
outside Varna.

Down sits the black-bearded gardener,
God the Father
with the planets in his basket,
and bites into the full fruit.
After each mouthful
we're in a different phase of apricot,
in apricot time
quick as the passing of a scent.
Until the new moon
when Mirza the gardener
spits in a godly manner
the meteor of pit.

Behind the Door the World

They come, they go,
the handle nods,
the door sings, wind rushes through.
Adults arrive from the world
whose door has a silver handle,
aunts, uncles, grandmothers come in
bringing their smells,
their other-people voices,
loaded with amazement not their own,
with pockets full of curiosity.
Then they go
behind the door with a silver handle
and get locked away with a key.
And when there's a knock,
that means that they'll come
back out of their closet
just behind the door, where the house ends,
where guests and uncles
loiter, say nothing, wait
to be let in,
very still and all of them.
Each on his own hanger.

O Drawer!

Shelter for the sinful word,
o drawer, odyssey so vast,
made of oak, homeric!
You will be the coffin
that once served as a cradle,
sinister imagination's respite,
a hollow for words
written in whisper,
condemned for eternity under the table.
The table—that horned quadruped—
will carry you through the years
and one day
from a green hope
you keep hidden in the dark,
a golden autumn will fly out:
yellowed words, not mine.
O drawer made of oak, homeric,
knots sealed long ago,
fractured whorls!

All Around London

The yellow hands of bananas
stick out from under the awnings—
they're checking for rain.

And all around—London.
Neon comets sweep the streets
with tails
and through Piccadilly
cobalt and orange planets
roll like fortune.
Big Ben knocks over the used-up hours
into deep rumbling dungeons.

I wanted to find traces of little Dorrit,
the buttons of kind-hearted Peggotty,
to knock on Scrooge's door,
but here they ask me:
—are there still four seasons there—
—do mushrooms grow after the rain—
—does the Vistula flow—

Because here the Vistula
is a dry smudge of blue
on the map of memory.

Because here there are rains of tears
that cannot revive anything.

The yellow hands of bananas
stick out from under the awnings—
they're checking for rain.
And all around—London.

Ante-Bird—Scarecrow

A green-freckled pink
fans itself out.
Skin stripped
from an angel of the reeds,
a wickerwork of wings.
An old Vietnamese wind
brushes against its scales.
Scarer of
"crows and evil spirits,"
ancestor—ante-bird!—of Paul Klee,
when it faces the home hearth
it is dozing;
when it faces spirits, when it faces crows,
when it faces me
it sharpens
its predatory symmetries,
launches arrows
of well-aimed rustling.
Then even the crow's feathers
are shouting,
and waters
ripple from the fall
of mortally smitten demons.

Here I stand in front of him
in the British Museum,
in love with the ubiquity of magic,
peaceful and content
because he has just driven out of me
the last evil spirit,
flying now out the window
bareback on the London crow.

from *Amulets and Definitions*

1960

The Empty Places After

1.

Here had been a tall horizon: running like a cat across rooftops, leaping over chimneys. That street is no more. The horizon escaped into the fields, across the Vistula. What was left after buildings is sky—darker than the sky around it, like the wall beneath a removed picture. The pigeons out of habit fly higher up, and at night on the fourth floor of air the moon switches on.

2.

Night is an empty place after day. Darkness is two-dimensional. Only the distant barking of dogs from nearby villages reconstructs space. And again the lost distances ring out. If you were to go forward blindly, you would get just as far as standing there motionless. Anyway you will only pass through the darkness at dawn. But the dogs—signs of the watching versts—assure that not everything is yet lost.

3.

Empty places after someone tend never to be empty. They spread out in every direction, the area designated for the living isn't enough for them. The one who is no longer won't fit inside the tight circle embracing him in life. Since disappearing, he inhabits all places simultaneously, fills the most incomprehensible volumes. His elusive matter, his tangible spirit replaces all our paths, it becomes a mole in the black earth of our dreams. And only time dislodges him from the places he had overtaken. But even then the place isn't empty for an instant. After the existing memory, the substance of those who are gone, grows silent, their final residence is usually plowed for new orchards and new cemeteries. Someone else's orchards and cemeteries, not subject to our customs.

My Attempted Travels

—to Australia, Portugal,
the moon, Puerto Rico,
to everywhere I didn't go.
To the blue bellies of glaciers,
to the dead pit of a stone,
to the labyrinth of yellow cheeses,
which are mummies of milk
and setting suns of curds,
from the tropical interiors of radiators,
into the dead end of the shell's last whorl,
where the source of a hum is pulsing,
to the sublime of the sparrow's plume,
which is the leaf of the bird, the rung of ascent,
which writes the highest notes of chirping,
to the old gramophone's tender hearts,
which get broken, torn to shreds
beneath a black record.

All my life I've headed out to all these places
and always the wind blows off my hat
and carries it in a completely different direction.
So I am always chasing, all my life,
escaping hats.

The Migration of the Hangers

Losing their last garments
they fly to countries beyond the sky,
hangers, the last of the hangers,
those attending birds of closets.
With a wiry clangor
and wooden flapping
above us.

Below them a naphthalenosphere,
the panting breaths of wool,
our careful darning,
the last fastened button—

The hangers will escape,
dressed in panicked nakedness
along the highway of birds.

Let's watch from the domestic rubble,
overwhelmed and on our own,
how the hangers are suspended in air,
watch those further and further off—
we, the withered gestures,
extinct poses.

From the Mythological Encyclopedia

i. Burners

The aureoles of stovetops.
The kitchen's rings of hell.
The trained hoops of fire.
Red-hot bagels
eaten by rust.
Horseshoes of galloping pots.
The poker's lovers
grinding in the fire of damnation.
And we cook our roast
on their fervor.

ii. Faucet

The drops fall from the faucet—
seeds of a great water.
They measure with a steady ticking
oceanic time.
Sometimes the faucet sings,
and this is a siren song
known to sailors and sinks.

The ruler of floods drips
from hydraulic sources,
comes as a humble trickle
to the kitchen's service.

iii. Ashtray

Refuge for earthly remains
that exhausted their last smoke.
At the bottom hisses a crumble of fire,
unreconciled with ash.
And impregnated comets
fall down into the urn
filled with the dust of musings.

iv. Table

An old table—
knock three times
on the unpainted wood—
descendant of wooden deities
with a sacred beetle in its womb.
Knock three times
against spells and complications,
to bless the full platter.
Here under the electric Holy Ghost

the haunted table,
tree against its will transformed,
matter chained in the stocks of usefulness,
stretched across itself with nails,
more man than wood.
Old table—
knock three times.

v. Cone

Spruces came flocking
bringing their cones,
each one covered
with green scales hung
by its tail on a branch.
This is the fish,
the green fish eternal,
that hangs and sings
sap-filled carols.

vi. Candle

Above each pious candle
a drop of gold
hangs by a black hair,

lined with sky-blue.
A storm of mosquitos
hatches from each candle
while processions of wax
run down,
fall into shadow.
And the devil lays claim
only to the candle-stub.

Thursday

In the very middle of the week there grows a Thursday the color of dust. On our stairs this is the painlessly creaking place, the smoothness of handrails worn slippery by generations of hands. This is the mouse under the cupboard that died awhile back, and nothing came of it. All the Thursday butterflies fade to nothing, the mirrors on Thursday repeat us, stammering until extinguished by a white yawn.

At the bottom of Thursday's lows, listless girls walk in crooked stockings. And the ghosts of cabbage soups languish in closed stairwells.

Thursday creeps under the yellow banners of flypaper, the choral keening of flies.

Those who forgot about Wednesday and have lost hope for Friday howl at the Thursday moon and pass on. For them, Thursday is eternal.

Inside-Out Views

The pink bellies of stones feed wetness to the ground. The underside of eagles, owls and sparrows, the embarrassing buttock of moon—my upturned monarchy: views of the other side visible to a dog's nose.

There you unleash your dog—who throws himself into the water and fetches, bringing you back the hunted horizon in his mouth. There peace and the right to exist are ensured by mimicries and simulations. The most an inhabitant of greenery can permit himself is a red liver.

What pretends to be death dresses in a rigid inertia. What pretends to be nothingness sinks into the background. What pretends to be predation—clawly hawks. There—underneath, on the other side—are the colors that remain in the last shelter of things not subservient to compromise. They're being overgrown by a cataract of civilized instincts.

Only occasionally wind scatters the fur of the common and reveals for a single gust a dazzling protozoa of colors.

May they be praised, the gray-winged guardian angels of Mimicry. Under each feather they carry a speck of the truthful rainbow.

Paris! Paris!

All reds come in the shape of lips. Even—s'il vous plaît—our shy little Mazovian cherries. So let us write with a promiscuous tongue and instead of a period—make a lip print. At the railway station in Radom we have a beer, and the world seen through a full mug is yellowed with the fear of Van Gogh, and a mug—mon Dieu!—also has no ear. Paris! Paris! Oy da dana, da dana!

We climb atop our dresser monuments and dream up the symbol of the New Avant-Garb: The Straight Line, which is a stem, and at its end hangs a lip-colored cherry. Oh, sweet drop of Marseillaise, little planet of our malignancy, flow down, drop into our thin borschts!

We geometricians of form, furrow-jumpers into others' imaginations, are waiting for you. And let the folks sing along: Paris! Paris! Oy dana, da dana!

Entomology

Yellow buzzes, and sharpened
on the light is honey's sting.
Gray whispers—the fire's fur.
The hymenoptera hours revolve
around an oil lamp eternity
in the music of late spheres.
Smoking azurely,
more and more lightly
such a blizzard circling,
such a maze, such a mazurka,
as if the prince of the beetles
were playing his own mustache.
A shameless flight, a swirl
will expose color—
tone after tone,
astride a breeze.
And in the hexagon
of beeswax—
the Eye of Instinct.
It knows everything.
It knows about nothing.

from *Picture Alphabet*

1962

Picture Alphabet

The forty-first century looked at me.
I came here after Champollion
into this land of articulated silence
into the country of unsignifying cicadas,
into the hieroglyphic whispers of the deserts
awakened, torn from the egyptian darkness.

The signs began moving across the sands of millennia,
dragging long harnesses of resurrected meanings.
The bird didn't sing in the air, it became a syllable.
The camel rid itself of highness, it became a syllable
to drag to us the corpse of Pharaonia.

Time to rest, signs, dwarfed and ill at ease since
the beginning of the alphabet, come back again,
birds, make cries, fluttering, birds birdlike again.
Lizards, flicker through millennia
as green lightning—flash lizardlike again
in your time eternal and quicker.

Charmed into unambiguity, enslaved into meaning
run from the desert into panic and evanescence.

Says the letter:
Before I became a syllable, I was.
I was a bird, not a word, I sharpened feathers
    on the wind.
I was allowed color and changeability.
I was imprisoned in sign. Let me out!
I'll take flight from papyrus perches,
I'll sit in your palm, when I am again,
I'll go back to bird speech.

Says the letter:
I was a lizard, one of those
that nests in the crevices of stone.
Thieves of the pyramids caught me,
thinking I was an emerald.
I knew the twisted ways of the reptile.
Now what's given to me is living
in a straight line in a chain of marks.
And I don't even know the rattle
of my own link.

Says the letter:
I was a fisherman. I understood
the heavy silence of fish,
the unyielding quiet of nets
all the way to the bottom of the Nile.
Today I myself am speechless.
I have no mouth,
I am the shape of a foreign sound.

    I say:
I was a letter, a sign, a sound,
a small number in a forged bill,
a stitch sewn with a too-thick thread.
I sat in the shadow of punctuation marks.
I was an expression flattened into whiteness
in the shop window of vainglorious fashions.
Ever since I returned, alone, to myself,
I let signs out from their purgatory
into the depths of their roots, their pre-being,
I restore breath to fossils,
and to silence—the cry that begot it.
I follow the lines of your hand
into the persias of fortunetelling, a nomad
reaching the rosy dawn of your fingernails
where, at the edge of barbarian night,
from the alphabets,
from the algebras and emblems, from signposts,
signs which only mean themselves
fly in again, fleeting and feathery.
And egypt ground to dust and sand
closes its night, blinded
by the sticky sweetness of a kiss.

Revolt

Captive objects,
obedient four-legged views
imprisoned by my glances,
limp by on their hind legs,
trampling their own lairs.

The utensils line up in order,
the mirrors
dressed up every day
keep silent about my sharp incisors.

Meekness furtively creeps by,
kind-heartedness loiters
at imaginary hearths.
Loftiness tiptoes.

And when they stand behind,
unleashed from the chains
of sensible reasons
and intended results—
they take an aim at me
and tread upon their own simulations.

Their sabbath is always at my back.

And a rose kills me with its club,
a star burns me,
and the breath of a bird
knocks me down
from my haughty constructions.

I Dreamt Myself

I dreamt myself. Far outside me.
From then on I began to exist—I met with myself,
carrying with me in the middle of the day
the starry key of a night not mine.
Before that I'd only happened to occur:
my own shadow
pretended to confirm me.
Now farewell. I won't
see myself anymore:
buried so far outside me
in layers of unfriendly day
by the opening of eyes and a yawn.

Fish on the Sand

From the waters that inertly
parted,
the gasping fish
thrown ashore
extinguishes, kindles
its pink gills,
pierces into us the hobnail
of its silver eye.

Let's kill it
with a silent knife.

So it won't wake us up
on the bank of night
with its howling.

Six Etudes

i. Old Beggar at the Church

At the gates of the church
deaf as the stump
of a felled tree
is a polychromed beggar
with an empty hand
He used to wear gold on his head
but it silvered
he had archangel wings
they turned into a hunchback
He scrapes together pennies
for the bell
so that God
might listen better

ii. Cemetery Squirrels

Squirrels
like cemeteries
the dead are good

they don't pick nuts
For their souls
squirrels
gravely
count
with prayerful paws
under the flames
of red tassels
hazelnut rosaries

iii. Gordian Bow

Who are you
bow
I am
a flowering knot
I intimidate
macedonian blades
and the cutters of ribbons
I withhold
from my own self
the easiness of my solutions
Pollinated by a spider
I bear fruit
I change into
a pom-pom

iv. Since Carp

Ever since carp went deaf
as a result of
constantly being in water
they know
man is mute
They sympathize with him
with a funereal fin
And ceaselessly
like a spindle
on the looms of their ponds
they weave water
they weave water
so as not to shred it
as people do
rain

v. Erotic

Behind the short-lived
screen
of the bat
you throw off
your last color
die out
in the hiss of a tear

you sink into
the infrared
before the flutter of my wings
blows you out
spark

vi. All the Same

Everything to me
is all the separate
the smoke
chopped off from the fire
the jar
broken off from the handle
and this tree after tree after tree
but still no forest
until the night comes
which unites
And then finally
everything to me
is all the same

from *The Bird Beyond the Bird*

1968

Today a Long Time Ago

I'm opening the door now
thirty years ago

Today I found the key

I meet you by the window
thirty years ago
You haven't been waiting long
You're just now young

I must prevent
everything that's happened

Only the future
can't be undone

Life

Already there are plants
already they are blooming
Then it's our turn
Then theirs again

We've stopped in
only for a moment
Flowers are older than us
It's not youth but the speed of plants
that confuses us

Unmoving green
outruns the reds
of our blood

If we meet
it will be here
it will be now
between the green
and the green

Penetration

I'm not ashamed of tears
I am the undresser of the onion
taking off her oniony scales
from the gold
violet
green
down to the deep leukoma
in search of
onion
onio
on
And here it turns out
there is no onion at all
and to such an extent
that even the inside
of the multilayered surface
lacks a space
for emptiness

From Fingerprints

Sharpen memory
until it pricks

Conjure you
from these whorled labyrinths
of touch that
knew you blindly

Gather you into a shape
from the maze of a rotating membrane
like a record needle
collects
all the music

Silently you come back
to every finger
of my hands

My Unsurvivor

In memory of Bruno Schulz

For so many years now
in my entresol of wooden beams
between the ceiling and the hall
25 watts of everlasting light
obscured by fly droppings glimmer
behind a barricade of old papers

There he is winding his watch
he doesn't brush away the spiders he sleeps

By now he must have deciphered every wood-knot
his still shadow overgrown by plaster
sometimes he's not there
even after curfew
he spends time in Hyderabad
unlocks the next knot
goes back further and further into the wood

Today my dream
knocked on wood for him

Mr. Bruno it's all right now
you can come down

But he waits for the unwaitforable
he cannot hear my dream
he, nobody
saner than anybody
he knows there's no entresol
nor light
nor me

Apocrypha of the Original Apple

Verily it is the Apple that
wants to be eaten
the Apple of sweet ignorance
of good and evil
a dappled appley appleton
it sways
squeezed into itself like a fist
until hurt by its own seeds

Quickly it revolves
around its own impatience
so that eve might have
all the blushing at once

And sayeth the Apple
verily I am the Apple
that wants to be eaten
to know your tongue
your teeth the roof of your mouth
Taste me let it be
as moses commanded

However from beneath her eyelids
eve devours the Sight of the Apple

and by winking divides
its nourishing blushes
into bites
she doesn't touch the Apple
filled to the tips of her lashes
by its red cry

And the Apple insane
flies off the branch
And eve falls
under the apple's blow

Papusza

If I hadn't learned to write, stupid me,
I'd be happy.

Papusza's confession

It's not the forest anymore
but too far to the world

She closed the pine's creaking door
She's not home

I was lithe
as a forest squirrel
even though I was
black

Now she is fainting
in every direction against the wind
A dry branch above her

All of her poverty
was the property
she lavishly stole
Everything from someone else's hen house

but the song
For that she stole letters
torn from newspapers posters signboards
she strung such beads of words
for no one

In dreams she had her own pine trees
They uprooted them
She stumbles over the holes

They unraveled her colors
not for darning
not for charming
and no shawl will come from it

The elements closed in on themselves
water drowned in water
fire burned in fire
the earth was buried in earth

Her song ran off beyond the forest
echoing
They will go slit its throat

Blackbearded they go
with a knife in the bootleg
with an aiming eye
with a curse hissing in their pipe
The whole gypsy forest

of nocturnal horse stealers
set out to meet her
tiny as a goldfinch
the shadows of ancestors
ran through
the crunch of brushwood

The pine forest
has only needles for her
The crackling gold cones
have settled into ash
Her little brothers
forest bird-brothers
went silent to deny her
The moon flew above
to give her away

She was lithe
as a forest squirrel
even though she was
black

She ran away from herself
and won't be back
She closed the pine's creaking door
She isn't anywhere
She wanted to bury
her song alive
to throw the letters into an anthill

Now the ants carry them along a blade of grass
A bird stutters
her last note

It's not the forest anymore
but too far to the world

So she goes low to the ground
the black squirrel from above
not to anywhere
nowhere
no one's

Creator

At dawn he created vast fogs
the size of his boredom

Above the waters he established night
the color of dirt under a fingernail

So go visit his world
wide as a yawn
Get in through the triumphant gate
Ring the great bell
three times

for this night condemned to eternity
for the fog that rots time
for the water struck speechless

Because the green kingdom of frogs
is not of his world

Frogs are of their own

And so he must croak
all by himself
in the nonexistent rushes

Traduction

For Helen Rubinstein

They translated him
into Parisian

His crab apples
swelled up into oranges

Through the wallhebeathisheadagainst
they drilled tunnels

His blunders
were rounded into reverences

From his ashes
rose a phoenix of face powder

His effusive rivers
closed in themselves

His barren cry
laid the egg of a note
and perched on a musical bar

His love
hélas
his wingèd love
buzzes
on the flypaper
of lipsticks

Tell How It Was

So yes I took part
it was the war then it wasn't
I came out of the camp
deloused and free

so the stars above me
were too many
out of habit I was
delousing the sky
once they multiply
good god won't give a nod
you'll have to throw
the whole sky away

so they were saying about me
oh he came out of the forest
but I did not come out
it was the forest that went away
hey boys
I'm standing shod with axes
standing still in the clearing
in the monotonous rhythm of a march
when was that

I'd have to ask Staszek
but he's dead
I don't want to bother him

so maybe I'm left with
some pine needles
a cap untouched by fire
eaten by moths
and all of our guys
not standing in the clearing
it's the forest that stands above them
twenty-something years old
I don't want to remember
just like they can't

so do not ask what else and how
I came out of this in one piece
let's say in almost one piece
that's it
there's nothing to talk about

The Bird Beyond the Bird

Look
the bird is escaping from itself
by flapping
it's bursting out of the nest of being
it wants to take a break from feathers
to slip out of being a bird

But it's unable
to outpace itself
by even a bird's beak

Look
the bird defeated
along with its inseparable self
lands on a branch

The bird on a branch
sings in every direction
reaching for seven echoes
simultaneously
moves through contradictory distances

Look
the bird victorious
throughout the forest

The bird beyond the bird

from *A Reading of Ashes*

1979

*   *   *

I was unable to save
a single life

I couldn't stop
a single bullet

so I circle cemeteries
that aren't there
I search for words
that aren't there
I run

to the aid uncalled for
to the rescue delayed

I want to get there on time
even if it's already over

The Assumption of Miriam
from a Street in Winter, 1942

incalculable snow was coming down
shreds of the sky were falling

thus she was ascending
passing motionlessly
white after white
a gentle height
after height
in the Elijah's chariot
of humiliation

above the fallen angels
of snows
into the zenith of frost
higher and higher above
hosanna
raised
to the lowest

5 VIII 1942

In memory of Janusz Korczak

What did the Old Doctor do
riding to treblinka
in a cattle car on the 5th of August
over a few hours of blood flow
over the dirty river of time

I don't know

what did the voluntary Charon do
ferryman without an oar
did he give the children the remains
of his winded breath
and leave for himself only
shivers in the bones

I don't know

did he lie to them for instance
in small numbing
doses
picking from their sweaty heads
the skittish lice of fear

I don't know

but then but later but there
in treblinka
all the terror all their tears
were against him

oh it was only
so many minutes that is a whole life
is that a lot or a little
I wasn't there I don't know

suddenly the Old Doctor saw
the children becoming
old like him
older and older
they had to catch up to the grayness of ash

so when he was hit
by an askar or ss man
they saw how the Doctor
became a child like them
smaller and smaller
until he was not born

since then on together with the Old Doctor
there are plenty of them nowhere

I know

The Six-Year-Old from the Ghetto Begging on Smolna Street in the Year 1942

she had nothing
but eyes she hadn't yet grown into
inside them quite by chance
two stars of David
that a tear might extinguish

so she wept

Her speech
was not silver
worth at least
some spit a turn of the head
her weeping speech
full of hunchbacked words

so she stopped speaking

Her silence
was not gold
worth at most
5 groszy maybe a carrot

a very polite silence
with a Jewish accent
of hunger

so she died

The Jews Left

she got a wardrobe dresses
still had time to go out of
though they'd go out of fashion anyway

an armchair from which someone once
got up for a moment and that
was enough for the rest of his life

platters pots full of hunger
but they'll be useful
for filling up

a portrait of a slain girl
in living color

she could still get that black table
in good condition
but it didn't look right

a little sad somehow

The Execution of Memory

When the first patches of snow
thaw
boots squish
in the swamp
near town

the black procession
of the graybearded Hasidim
are coming back

I recognize old Apcie

crows spell out loud
the twigs of Hebrew
verses

Here once stood a synagogue
with the birds' bell tower of poplar

Branches raised up
like arms
greet a salvo of silence
and the killed memory
falls

a leafless skeleton of shadow
on its back

and the sudden flow of time
bleeds snowmelt again

A Gathering of Stones

For Bronisław Anlen

The stones are gathering

And who was to come here
When there is stone upon stone
it means they're acquainted

Here a stone says
kaddish
with its weight
its multitude
and stones the place
in the painless grass

The stones are gathering

Here sometimes an old man
will lug inside him
feldspar quartz and burden
and a wisp of green
bloodied with a rose

he will place it exactly
anywhere knowing

that he's put it right into the hands
of his daughter Rachel
because here everywhere are the hands
of his daughter Rachel

And even if it's Miriam who gets the flower
so be it she also deserves
a petal of memory
even by mistake

The old man goes away
A stone stands up

The End of the Rite

The seven-branched poplar
was blown out by the wind
the downed sparks of leaves
go out

A soot of crows
smokes into a cloud

from *Illicit*

1979

I'll Tell You a Story

I'll tell you a story
before it emerges cleansed from us
that is from sand
quite well preserved
like the skeleton of a plesiosaur
under the gobi desert

I'll tell it still warm
from the furnaces of auschwitz
I'll tell it still frozen
from the snows of kolyma
a history of dirty hands
a history of hands severed

it's not in the textbooks
in order not to dirty
the white spots
on the map of the time and times

I'll tell you a story
the unheard one
that seldom arrives
for the exhumation of dreams

my proof is a silence
shot clean through
that's why I speak in a whisper
I'll tell a story

But don't repeat it

Illicit

It's dark
between us
a blackwash of darkness
although the white day
clatters against stone
like a blind man's cane
so I carry your cry
though it's slashed
by the criss-cross of bars
To your hungers
I throw bread
that the birds will eat

I defend you
by groping
rescue you in the dark
will find you hit or miss
will pass you by mistake

where you're watching
still burning
where you're sleeping
where you have died

*   *   *

In memory of Max Brod who, breaking
Kafka's will, didn't burn his manuscripts

With a temperature of 101.3
and an exile's traveling bag
here comes
the old cough
cured out of Franz Kafka

It drowns out the manuscripts
spared from
fire's kindness

And whispers Max
I forgive you Only
what to do with this
hundred-volumed silence

Max my Max
burn this my silence

Gdańsk Train Station, Warsaw 1968

In memory of Arnold Słucki

Departing Now departing
Get on Close the doors please
Departing for the sunken islands
down beneath the dried up seas

there in the heart's chamber
get on close the doors please
he'll meet his death overdue
blend into its crowd
delayed just him

farewell Arnold

and he waves from the window
of a suddening distance
first only with a handkerchief
and now with the sky
in which a cloud lingers on
above us and stays

and we unreturnably remain

The Hour Is Ripe

It's night the hour is ripe
let's go kill the dead

If something or other is left
we'll turn it into nothing or less

if a bone is left
we will deny it

if they ascended to heaven
we'll send tall birds
to peck them dead on high

if their word their gesture
dwells among us
we'll install
faulty memory conductors

if what's left of them is just a sign
we'll turn it into a trademark
like for example rat poison

if what's left of them is orphanhood
we'll sever their separation
in a family unification campaign

because the dead are contagious
because the dead are too eloquent
because the dead have nothing
to excuse us for

It's night the hour is ripe
let's go kill the dead

we cannot leave them
prey to eternity

Recipe

First we raise
angkor temples
stone is grown
in our own image
millennia are gathered
the books of books are multiplied
and man is born
each one separately
this takes time
it has to take time

what comes next occurs more swiftly

we set the temple on fire
from the statues from the columns
the chipped stone is extracted
millennia get knocked down
letters are plucked alive from books
or sunken at the bottom of the tonlé-sap

we must quickly undo
the centuries of centuries
the era is not particular
and has no time to lose
it has us to lose

1977

The Rite

where St. Sebastian
accurately covered
with arrow-feathers
receives wings
to fly away
high into salvation

there an archer with the squinting eye
of improvidence
plucks his lute-string
holy
holy
holy

How to Spoil the Cannibals' Fun

I've been thinking a long time
about how to spoil
the cannibals' fun

wait until they
cook themselves
beneath the gold lid of sun
but they're immune
to being cooked

don't give in to
being eaten
this program is a bit austere
and not quite realistic
once they've already got you
on their tongues

eat them instead
now that would be
distasteful

then maybe make people
disgusting to them
but how could we

and so they sit
in their comfortable jungles
with a mouthful
of humanity

from *Errata*

1981

Childhood, 1940

sooner would a crow turn white
than Poland be Poland again
we were told and also
that the Lord God had gone away
as far as america
and wouldn't be back

in train cars
from hooks from nails
we girls tongued the frost
and then the boys
who were too young to live
buried in the snow
in those coffins

that crept back up
to the surface
on easter
and that needed
a second burial

which is why we looked out
through the spyglass of icicles
to see if from behind all those siberias
the Lord God hadn't come flying
on his white crow

A Certain Dickens

a certain dickens more questionable
than the ghost of Marley
chases his debtor Micawber
clings to Peggotty's buttons

Little Dorrit asks him
mr dickens why
didn't you write yourself
it would have been good for you
you're so pale she says
that you're not even there

and she can't help him
in any other way
than by performing
her own rite
of being

Ringelblum Archive
(Oneg Shabbat)

and I am woken
by the posthumous cry of Saturday
signed up
in tiny letters
to speak
after the last salvo

from *Death of a Unicorn*

1981

Incantation

o water that takes your own
shape
when you are very small
o single-celled
your name is a drop
you persist from high to low
not knowing a vessel
o closed-within-yourself
you perish when you open
and you'll give birth to the sea
and be greeted
by salt and dolphin and columbus
and by susanna wallowing
her hair in rainwater
o droplet with nothing
to differ you from droplet
hollower of stone

Getting Out of the Mirror

The mirror peeping at me
the suspect
is all surface
about me it doesn't have
the best reflection

And I have intentions
left and right
high and low
but it keeps me
in its rectangular stocks

with gilded flattery
it dresses me in a countenance
it rococos
arms me with a gesture

I get out of its depths
onto my shore
I shake off
two drops
of similarity
and head out to meet
unrepeatable views

A flood of swollen mirrors
laps at my heels
and throws the jellyfish
of someone else's eyes
onto the sand

*　　*　　*

in the steep evenings of falling asleep
an oblique line under the door
from the parents' room
crossed out bad dreams
with a gold stroke

that room expired long ago
and so did the parents
the blown-up dream
flew away as cloud

I managed to bring
only this gold footbridge
to cross in unexpired
sometimes
from darkness into darkness

Don't Be Surprised

Don't be surprised
that he draws stubbornly amusing hope
from old calendars
the bible of harlequins
that he tosses bait
for the fish of the zodiac
between the low tide of fear
and the high tide of pain
that he believes in copper
in the power of water
in the grace of an afternoon
in the compassion of air
don't be surprised that he plays
a solitaire of salvation
and throws down
one fear after another
into the abyss
to make it more shallow

a falling icarus
grabs on even to a dragonfly

Tangolia, 1936

our little sicily of the woods
our summer tangolia
with a view of the postcards
from uncle cleophas
the soprano on the gramophone
My Charming Dream
if the weather permits
the storm will pass us by
lola is smelling the fresh air
oh her pointed breasts
unbutton with her breath
three buttons of her blouse
abram brought a fat hen
she died from swallowing a straw
so now for dinner
an oily-eyed broth
grandfather lengthens
his mustache with noodles
on the coffee table
an old catalog of agricultural machines
and saint jacek is a dead ringer for
the jack of clubs
if not for his glasses
grandfather would play whist with him

aunt gruszczyńska
hums an old song just the beginning
the rest she forgot
now how did it go
bah the late antoś would know
at night the matthiola smells
milk curdles
lola dreams

List of Telephone Subscribers for
the Capital City of Warsaw
for the Year 1938-39

For Rafael Scharf

After the sudden removal of precise addresses
to general onomastics
numbers returned to the abstraction of figures
and the body became the word
in the Armorial of Subscribers

Here are the authenticated chosen
who are No One on No Street
and they are still so precise
you could sidestep a puddle
with eyes closed
and cross
to that stand with kvass and pumpkin seeds

They crossed
and stand belatedly
in neat lines of printed letters
and everything is in order
alphabetical
on the lists of inattendance

And a deaf telephone calls them
and its black bell rings in empty places
for those who had once been caught
in the red-handed act
of living

There I'll Get Lost

if somewhere there survive
unpopulated spots
there I'll get lost
like adam
before he turned into humankind
among the flaming pillars of pines

there I'll get lost
a leafless relative of tamarisks
kin to the oriole
prodigal son of the beetle
where a thicket spreads
in my primeval garden

in the still barefoot mundane
in the hymnals of silence
up to the nest where the Holy Spirit
hatches the Word

Refuge

He speaks of transience
as if a faraway custom
of the ayub tribe
he has plenty of time

he built of it
an indigenous distance
and is the accountant of generations of birds
he collects their feathers
for an eternal pillow

only his guessing
leads him to the steep banks
where the distance constantly and abruptly ends
But he returns from those
bright promontories
unconverted
by the shamans of fear

he will endure much
he has himself in reserve

Slowness

Motionlessly I leave behind
the rush of the hot highways
I sit down low
by the forest
with legs in the cool grass

I've already been on time

it's my old hurry all on its own
now that stirs the dust
spins the wheels

I take possession
of my real estate
slowly I settle in
I occupy a leaf
water it with my sweat

here under a tin sky
welded by airplanes
where all the faraways
have long been aired
before in the late thicket
I sleep throughout the forest

*   *   *

My son, eat thou honey, because it is good; and
the honeycomb, which is sweet to thy taste
—Proverbs 24:13

Honey lives only
in hexagons for
they ensure it
a balance of sweetness

their shape is
a star's design
six
implied triangles
drinking from the center's source

shrouded in the most frugally
abundant capacity
in order not to lose
a single drop of space

until the heavenly beekeeper
licks his godly finger
pointing
to the golden core of flavor

nursed
into gentleness
by the violence of stings

Prayer to the Holy Louse

*It was in the spring of 1944, during
the delousing of the Gypsy barracks
in Auschwitz-Birkenau.*

skirts scarves
were withering in the delousing room
all in protective colors

in poppies in buttercups in daisies
in case of a meadow
that will never appear

a Gypsy in the bathhouse of birkenau
stripped of colors
with a clenched fist
clothed
in long folds of water

hid in her palm
a grain of life
a seed of escape
between the life-line
and the heart-line
at the crossroads
of chiromancy

concealed in her cupped hand
the last louse
which always leaves
when death arrives
the Gypsy was singing
in the bathhouse of birkenau

swanta dźuw
na dźa mandyr

holy louse
don't leave me
I will not let you go
I have only you
god doesn't come to hell

your sisters leave
our dead
stay with me
save me
holy louse

a guard ran up with a whip
pried her fingers open
What have you got there thief show me
this diamond
this coin this gold

And down fell the louse
and down fell the star

The empty hand remained
and the empty sky
And into it came
smoke after smoke
smoke after smoke

The Gypsy Road

I dedicate this to Papusza

Their black horse was killed
and so was their silver-maned road

oh there it lies
at crossroads with itself
decomposing in the heat

Wheels slick with mushrooms
had quietly ridden over it
while an earring replied
to the questions of the sun

Their black horse was killed
and so was their silver-maned road

So the Gypsies sold
every music from the violin
in the Wieliszewo market
because now there was nowhere
left to play

With their dog's sense of smell
they're escaping
to where on some fifth wheel
their fortune rolls

Village Landscape

There is silence in the meadows
of former battlefields

the bank of the bug river arranges
shells and bones

at times a wasp's ricochet
shoots from the burdocks

someone was buried here
or somewhere else

and there is no hole in heaven
as there is on earth

from *The Initial*

1994

The Initial

where the green snake at the bottom of a dark cellar
under the mossy cover of rumbling and wood
rolled around itself and unrolled from itself
like the intricate peeling whittled by a sword
from the sour planetoid of a royal apple
I didn't look under the lid didn't see the snake
but I knew him loop after loop
as he drank the wet spots as he grazed the darkness
and I understood down to the bottom after years
that like him on meanderings had slithered to nothing
that it was simply so tortuously
the venomous initial in my alphabet of dreams
and that in autumn it would be invisibly gold
and that it must have had a Latin name

Everything I Don't Know

Not a shred not a letter
and so it was begotten

leafing through suppositions
paginating wonders
in the covers remaining
after the ripped-out book

I don't remember the title

most likely subsumed by
the divine elephant on the cover
that carried me in a palanquin
to the parts of the world
where if something happens
it happens forever
where even if holy days are no more
holy moments persist

for sixty years I've been going
through seasons so capacious
that will house centuries of centuries
through colors so vast
that rainbows burst

for so many years I've scattered
wind-dusted words
so my book would grow back
the one ripped before me

that's how I write the unfound
in its pages
everything I don't know

.

The Road to Zuzela

and again I go through the woods to Zuzela

may everything be repeated like
the cuckoo's two-syllabled voice
known here only from being heard

they want to measure my future time
and from the cuckoo
lay a horoscope egg
so that it hatches
an unfledged destiny

my fear is weaving it a nest

I hear you cuckoo I won't listen
I'll pass you by I won't yet pass away
and again through the woods from Zuzela
I'll return to myself
immortal almost

From the Nature Notebook

1.

this unchanging landscape
with a lifelong birch
with the wind tugging at the tree
and leaving it in place
now he knows that on the other side
on the back side
is a darkness
where patiently
spiders hatch

2.

serene pigeons
with rainbows on their neck
are studded with feathers
one after the other

the arrow that grows out of us
doesn't hurt

3.

a dragonfly
divining rod of amazement
made of emerald-sapphire
with a pair of huge eyes
inflated with sight
rises on the transparent
illusion of wings

it will freeze suddenly
it will hold time like a breath

to rest for a moment
to test eternity
in the harbor of balance
in itself
in a dragonfly

4.

by their leaves you shall know them
said the Lord
and since then

by the cut of leaf
is expressed
a maple star
a poplar heart

5.

a far-reaching flower
speaks out loud
to blind moths
with scent

each in its own dialect

6.

a falling feather
lingers in the air

it still remembers the wing

7.

from branches a cap of snow falls
and leaves a trail
a trace of snow on snow

8.

in the trunks shot through by bird
the hollows are overgrown with silence

put out time go to sleep
put out time

don't burn it needlessly
it may come in handy
for the next part of the flight

My Belated Guests

My belated guests from the Tertiary of dream
long unwaited for still the same
come in take off their shoes not to dirty
the floors not to trample the silence
Welcome My Friends and I have nothing to say
to the question what's new other than yes
I heard the whine of the opening door
It's still happy like my old dog
when I'd return home
Please sit down, I never thought I would
see you once you died
it's nice that from your side from the other side
you're here though I feel silly
I'm still alive after you after time
as if nothing happened as if no one ever
so have some patience a moment of foreverandever
I have fees to pay to clean up after myself
to sleep to wake to sleep to wake and still
so much

Memorial

In a time when books die they must be written again
for no one from a habit lasting for millennia
If not earthward than skyward
like the mad Mr. Dick Miss Trotwood's advisor
who winged his manuscripts into kites
and castaway threw them into the blue ocean
into that godly fishery for nothing for the wind

Let them sink to the lowest of the heights the heavy words
that no one reads here because why and what for
fleeting memorials
prayers with no address

The Dot over the I

this star they say is inadvertently late
by a million and a half light years
a nice coincidence
how the pre-eternal
just today on Friday at three in the morning
managed at the last minute
to overlook me from on high
and to place above my existence
the delinquent dot.

Freedom

She arrived here from all directions
who would know her in such rain
this vagrant with this cardboard
with a scrawl in nondescript

betrayingly black-haired
swathed in the refuse of colors
of every flag in the world

she the transylvanian gypsy
in an encounter with the wind
crouches in the very middle of a sunday
assisted by turtledoves
the heaven-dwellers from her parts

she collects whatever she gets
and still doesn't have enough
for the seven wonders
for any old piece of bread

eventually she hurls the wind over her back
and disappears
not leaving even
a place behind her

Paired Inscription

1.

My gratitude to the wilderness
I wander so accurately
to fire that was for burning
but that warmed and made light
to errors that discover
more than I had lost
to my ignorance
which omits
only what is
not a whit more

2.

I am going out of date
someone has left again from everywhere
there's less and less proof of me
and now who will believe
in my ungrounded years
in truths so incorruptible
that they pay nothing back

from *Beforetime and Aftertime*

2004

Dear Zbigniew

I recreate in me
the poet from Pompeii
covered over
some time ago

I blow away the powdered lava
I cannot detect a pulse
and here dear Zbigniew
what comes into being
is my poem
not too bad
perfectly foreign

Absent

I who am absent ask
please turn off the text messages
stop licking stamps
don't call
starting today I have in me
too little of myself
I won't say a word
not a word

my word
my not a word
using this moment of inattention
has stopped to mean
I'm not looking for it

I who am absent
still understand
the fluid narrative of clouds

they fly and draw from themselves
the furthest-reaching

conclusions and consequences
across the sky

o cloud cloud and cloud
unlike yourself
the same

I'm Heading Out

After honors for catastrophes
paid for with gravestone weeds
after betrayals glorified
hopes unlearned
full of defeats
I've had enough

live on humanity
just try not to
catch a cold
not to write yourself off
wipe yourself out

meanwhile I'm heading out

One day I'll come back if I come back
I'll try to make it
by the end of the world

so just in case
save me
the place I leave behind

*   *   *

rivers suspend their current
abandon their beds
from one place to another
woods and wildernesses roam
no map can keep up
after them after us
squirrels from on high lose
the last bits of gravity
time is running faster
our history
won't fit in it now

Kazakhstan, USSR

they let us out of the wagons
right here

And nothing anywhere

not a river
to drown in

or a tree
to hang oneself

from "Side Notes"

roosters before day
buglers of premonitions
summon yesterday
to return

close the door
so that the unwelcome doesn't come in
light the lamp
so that the night knows its limits
who is speaking
no one
and I was thinking that

sometimes
at the end of August
the night will spill stars
but they always fall
far from here

oh this is where
elves and dwarves live
I guess I won't
drop in
they might not
be at home

everything
is heavier
than itself
that's why it falls

I am waiting
in case
something happens

something is waiting
in case
I

It's time now
it's
the end of ends

too bad
I hadn't even
gotten tired

I haven't yet domesticated
my dreams
so that I might
bring them out into the green daylight
from where
they go in herds

not that they're disobedient
although they are disobedient
but that I'm afraid of them
like blood is of a knife

the hum went over
the tips of the pines
it tossed down cones
ran off to get the rain

the sand lizard
so quick
is already
not where
it is

from *Pantarheia*

2006

By Itself

I preoccupy myself with walking
somehow it goes
sometimes it stumbles
I preoccupy myself with breathing
with sleeping with being
and earlier
all of it went by itself

I preoccupy myself with staying
balanced and once it
preoccupied itself with me

so I limp I flounder
in the wilderness of self-reliance
more and more
behind myself
in the back

neither to wait
or to catch up

to stay I guess

Aequinoctium

invited by my uncle's wife
to the equinox of day and night
I run, scaring off rabbits
seasons are punctual
I can't be late

the equinoctial housewife
bakes an eternally sad cake
she moans next to the hen
just now laying
a natural-sized egg

beyond the seasons of the world
and the directions of time
she sets the saffron day
with a heavenly rim
for a beyond-earthly meeting
of sisterly night
with brotherly day

so much effort for this one moment
that will pass more quickly
than it has time to appear
now she's only waiting
for the star to ring

good day night
good night day
greetings to uncle's wife

Wormwood Night

last night
around dawn maybe
I could smell through the window
the starless wormwood
as if its leaf were rubbed
between the fingers

she entered
the same way
and I didn't recognize her
although once
I knew her night

I didn't want to offend
the unremembered

she entered or maybe
only her voice
ooph, what a relief
my whole life behind me
I pretended not to hear
I'm afraid of sadness
the wormwood faded away

I turned over
to the other side
of life

Pantarheia

long ago in the Guam Archipelago
I met the Pantarheia
four-winged
with large slanted eyes
one
on each wing
not noted in Linnaeus

today she is flying to me
already halfway here
she hobbles in the airs
my three-winged one
asymmetrical
the Youppi typhoon
tore from her
the fourth wing

I keep it in this drawer
the left hazel one now asleep
careful
don't touch because
it's losing sight
and there
Youppi junior lurks

for one more sidelong glance
or maybe even three
slant-eyed

and you are flying after
your ruin or to
your ruin
who knows Pantarheia

you are halfway now
so many years and years
and years
only in flight and flight
and flight

oh how long it is
this halfway

Screening Cancelled

this dream on an ev-
en path
suddenly didn't reach the end
I intended to replay it
and now what

in rental stores they don't have it
in the public somnitech also no
there was only one copy
mine

all that's left is a bed sheet
the feature-length broke off
the ends went into the night
and I don't know
what comes later or before that
nor the would-be plots

I kept promising this dream
with an accompaniment
of Satie and a bumblebee
and now what
now nothing

I have to cancel
this screening this music
and this groundless
poem
I'm sorry bumblebee
forgive me Erik

We

we animals superior
by our own nomination
we with our disappearing
tail of instincts
because without them it's easier
to persist in our stubborn error

our opposition to nature
makes her itch
so she scratches herself and shudders
with a tsunami, for instance

then we die out a little
and those who remain
feel very sorry

Afterword

Jerzy Ficowski was part of the generation whose
teenage years were torn apart by the Second World
War. He was born in 1924 in Warsaw, into a Polish
intelligentsia family; his father Tadeusz Ficowski was
a linguist and philosopher. During the war and the
Nazi occupation of Poland (1939–1945) he fought in
the Resistance and, in 1944, took part in the Warsaw
Uprising. After the war he studied journalism, philos-
ophy, and sociology. He was a poet, an essayist, the
preeminent expert on and editor of Bruno Schulz, the
principal Polish scholar of Gypsy lore, a poetry trans-
lator, and—one of the most surprising omissions from
the so-called canon of the post-war Polish poets.

His first book of poems, *Ołowiani żołnierze*
(Lead Soldiers), appeared in 1948, his last, *Pantareja*
(Pantarheia), came out in 2006, a few months before
he died. Between these two there were thirteen
other poetry books, some of which—first in the
'70s, when Ficowski was a dissident, then in the '80s,
during martial law—were published by small emigré

presses in England and by underground publishers in Poland, illegal at the time. For much of his life, into the '80s, he earned his living as a popular songwriter, while publishing poetry and prose during periods of political thaws.

After the war he traveled with the Polish Roma, and became an avid historian of them, documenting their culture in several monographs: the first edition of his classic ethnography study, *Cyganie na polskich drogach* (Gypsies on Polish Roads) appeared in 1965, two revised and enlarged editions followed in 1985 and 2013. He also translated into Polish the songs and poetry of Papusza ("papusza" meaning "doll" in Romany) whose real name was Bronisława Wajs.

The other translations by Ficowski are no less inspiring. In 1958 he published a selection by Federico García Lorca, reprinted every decade, and still unsurpassed. His perfect translations of the Russian poems by young Bolesław Leśmian (the best Polish poet of the twentieth century), Ficowski's life-long love in Polish poetry, indicate how "complete" a poet Leśmian was from the start. Ficowski also translated and edited the only Polish anthology of folk Yiddish poets, as well as an anthology of Romanian folk poetry, a masterpiece of poetry translation into Polish. The complete list would be too long.

Among his many books, there is one called *Wspominki starowarszawskie* (Memories of Old Warsaw, 1959), based on stories told by people in dying professions still active in the nineteenth century; and another called *Bajędy z augustowskich lasów* (Stories from the Augustów Woods, 1998), based on anecdotes told by people from the Augustów region. And there is also one of a different sort, *W sierocińcu świata* (In the Orphanage of the World, 1993, 1996), a monograph on Witold Wojtkiewicz, one of the great neglected Polish painters, who died in 1909 before he turned thirty.

Ficowski was a very independent and original mind. He discovered some of the most exciting ingredients in Polish culture before others even realized they were there. These he brought to the public eye, showing their subversive potential. They were unlicensed and under the radar, existing on the margins and marginalized, things that the monumental Polish mainstream was not ready for or did not have time to notice. Had it not been for his eye and sensibility, much of what he discovered and wrote about, and learned from as a poet, would have been irretrievably lost. Without Ficowski's care and discoveries Polish culture would be much poorer today.

Apart from Leśmian, his other great literary love, whom he also never met, was Bruno Schulz, the master of Polish prose, killed in the Drohobych ghetto in 1942. Ficowski devoted decades of his life to searching for Schulz's letters and drawings, editing them as well as his prose, and writing about him. His most important book on Schulz was *Regiony wielkiej herezji* (1967, the final enlarged edition published in 2002). The shorter version of the monograph appeared in America as *Regions of the Great Heresy* in 2000, translated by Theodosia S. Robertson. Ficowski is known, too, as editor and commentator in several American editions of Bruno Schulz's prose.

Ficowski was also one of the last in the line of great twentieth-century Polish poets writing ingenious poetry for children, regularly producing collections over several decades. In 1970 he published a book of oneiric short stories, *Czekanie na sen psa* (reissued in 1987 and 2014), a contemporary classic of the genre. It appeared in English relatively recently as *Waiting for the Dog to Sleep*, from Twisted Spoon Press in 2006, translated by Soren A. Gauger and Marcin Piekoszewski.

Meanwhile his greatest claim to fame in Polish, his poetry, didn't attract much attention in America, largely because the map had been drawn by Czesław Miłosz, whose influential 1960s anthology of Polish poetry (revised and enlarged a few times through the '80s) excluded Ficowski. Except for a few poems in two or three anthologies conceived with a political theme, American translators toed the line, banishing Ficowski to the Siberia of good intentions. His was the role of the good man, the resistance fighter, movingly involved in battles for the right causes. Wasn't he full of sympathy for Jews and Gypsies, and for simple people, revealing his specific ethnographic interests, and involvement, in things of limited importance? He was dogged by this attitude toward him his entire life. That he was also a member of the dissident KOR group, that he signed letters of political protest, and that he was banned like other dissidents, somehow didn't cut it. An independent aesthetic that demands homework tends to be problematic. In his aesthetic "offness" and strong singularity, Ficowski set a great example.

That is certainly one reason why only a brief book of Ficowski's poems in English (barely thirty pages) has ever appeared, forty years ago. It was the translation of *Odczytanie popiołów* (1979), a sequence of twenty-odd short poems, preoccupied with the annihilation of Jews during the war. The poems were written over the course of more than twenty years, slowly, not as a "project." Ficowski published individual poems on this theme in various volumes, two or three in each, as they were written, a kind of ongoing meditation in verse, until they constructed the sequence. *A Reading of Ashes*, as it was called in the English translation of Keith Bosley and Krystyna Wandycz, came out in 1981 from The Menard Press in London. It was fortunate that the sequence was in print when Daniel Weissbort published his anthology *The Poetry of Survival* (1992). Without Ficowski, it would have been much thinner.

Apart from their obedience to the taste-makers of the time, American translators had another reason for avoiding Ficowski. Translationwise, out of Ficowski's contemporaries known in America, two (each for different reasons) seem particularly difficult: Miron Białoszewski and Wisława Szymborska. Even in that context, however, Ficowski seems more complex to translate. Somewhat like Leśmian, his great predecessor and inspiration, Ficowski is a poet of local lore and myths, most inventively and most radically rooted in the phraseology of the Polish language, reaching into it with a particular Ficowskian imagination and discipline, fusing past speech with its current forms. This inspired expertise, together with his concept of time—both past and present—produces a stunning effect in the original. That is perhaps the aspect of his poetry which seems dominant today, when the excesses of some political writing are still so freshly remembered. And this, his treatment of time and language, is what makes him such an important figure to discover.

These specific characteristics of the original do not occur in isolation. On the contrary: they are the constant background of the "thematic" events, although to divide the thematic events from the adventures of the language would be risky business in Ficowski's poems. The linguistic incidents are part of the "subject matter," and are as important as some of the most understandable stories that the poems tell.

Of course we are bound to miss nuances in translation, especially given that the structure of Polish is so different from that of English. One particular example, nevertheless, may demonstrate something of the characteristic Ficowskian system (or characteristic Ficowskian language), even in translation. It's the neologism "Pantareja" ("Pantarheia" being the English version), the title of his last book, which fuses in this one word his main interests, the linguistic and the chronological. Ficowski built his new noun out of Heraclitus' famous sentence *panta rhei* (everything changes). The noun did not exist before, but now it will. In the text of the poem "Pantarheia," the title poem of the book, Ficowski broadens the concept of time through the imaginary metamorphosis of nature, and we see how (naturally) all things connect in their mutual affections. And perhaps how, thanks to the mental rhyme which occurs in Polish (*Pantareja – Odyseja*), his short narrative instantly connects to the ancient epic.

All this is to say that translating Ficowski's poetry more extensively into English would have been a serious challenge anyway, even without toeing the line. With his linguistic adventurousness, with his way of combining the local, the historical and the public, the ethnic and the personal, and with his deep understanding of how meaningful intonation can be, he will always be a translators' nightmare.

Toward the end of his life, younger poets began to appreciate what Ficowski did, and how indispensable he had been in his efforts. A lot of new thinking, and better understanding, has gone into what has been written about him since he died.

The problem that Ficowski's poetry poses for translators (like his contemporary Białoszewski's) is that those who have the strongest impact on other poets and on the language of poetry are often those whose writing is so embedded in their language that they "do not translate." And what does not translate, or what translates badly, does not do any good—neither to the poet translated nor to the language where the poet got dragged by some well-wishers. Who knows what we have done. Our choice here was limited to what seemed translatable enough and what—after six or seven years of our slow efforts—we decided did translate well enough. This was what we could live with, out of a life's work of poetry that is hardly translatable, and yet was written by one of the most original Polish poets writing in the twentieth century.

Piotr Sommer
4 iv 20

BIOGRAPHICAL NOTES

JERZY FICOWSKI was born on September 4, 1924 in Warsaw. During the occupation he was a soldier in the Home Army and took part in the Warsaw Uprising. After the war, he studied journalism, philosophy, and sociology. One of the most original Polish poets of the 20th century, he published fifteen volumes of poetry, beginning with *Ołowiani żołnierze* (Lead Soldiers) in 1948. His wanderings with Polish Roma at the turn of the 1940s and 1950s resulted in the monograph *Cyganie na polskich drogach* (Gypsies on Polish Roads, 1965) as well as translations from Romany of the poet Papusza. His interest in Jewish history and culture resulted in an anthology of folk poetry of Polish Jews, *Rodzynki z migdałami* (Raisins with Almonds, 1964). He also translated into Polish poetry from the Romanian, Spanish, and Russian. His lifelong fascination with the writings of Bruno Schulz started during the occupation. He later researched and collected materials about Bruno Schulz, finding and publishing many of Schulz's unknown manuscripts, prints, and drawings. Ficowski's pioneering biography and analysis of Schulz's work is *Regions of the Great Heresy* (1967). In the '70s and '80s Ficowski was banned from printing and published in underground editions. His last volume of poetry, *Pantareja*, appeared in 2006, a few months before his death.

JENNIFER GROTZ is the author of three books of poetry, *Window Left Open* (Graywolf Press), *The Needle* (Houghton Mifflin Harcourt), and *Cusp* (Mariner Books) as well as translator of two books from the French: *Psalms of All My Days* (Carnegie Mellon), a selection of Patrice de La Tour du Pin, and *Rochester Knockings* (Open Letter), a novel by Hubert Haddad. She teaches at the University of Rochester and directs the Bread Loaf Writers' Conferences.

PIOTR SOMMER is a Polish poet, the author of *Things to Translate* (Bloodaxe Books), *Continued* (Wesleyan UP), and *Overdoing It* (Trias Chapbook Series). He has published poetry collections, books of essays on poetry, and poetry translations (Ashbery, Berryman, Cage, Koch, Lowell, O'Hara, Reznikoff, Schubert, Schuyler). He has won prizes and fellowships, and has taught poetry at American universities. He lives outside Warsaw and edits *Literatura na Świecie*, a magazine of foreign writing in Polish translations.

ACKNOWLEDGMENTS

Grateful thanks to the Jerzy Ficowski Foundation.
Thanks also to the editors and journals in which
many of these translations previously appeared, some-
times in slightly different forms:

American Poetry Review: "The Hour is Ripe," "List
    of Telephone Subscribers for the Capital City
    of Warsaw for the Year 1938-39," "I'll Tell You
    a Story," "From the Nature Notebook"
Arkansas International: "The Initial," "Getting Out
    of the Mirror"
Copper Nickel: "Penetration," "The Bird Beyond
    the Bird," "Thursday," "Entomology," "Creator"
Cortland Review: "Behind the Door the World"
Gulf Coast: "Inside-Out Views," "Tell How It Was"
Image: "*** (Honey lives only)," "Prayer to the Holy
    Louse," "The Assumption of Miriam from a
    Street in Winter, 1942," "Apricot Time," "A
    Gathering of Stones," "The Six-Year Old from
    the Ghetto Begging on Smolna Street in the
    Year 1942"
Kenyon Review: "O Drawer," "Incantation"
The Nation: "Paris! Paris!"

New England Review: "My Attempted Travels,"
   "Revolt"
New York Review of Books: "*** (With a temperature of 101.3)"
Parnassus: "Traduction"
Ploughshares: "Apocrypha of the Original Apple"
PN Review: "Six Etudes"
Poetry: "August 5, 1942" ("5 VIII 1942")
Poetry International: "The Dot over the I," "From the Mythological Encyclopedia," "Kazakhstan, USSR," "Migration of the Hangers," "Don't Be Surprised," "From Fingerprints"
Raritan: "Dear Zbigniew," "Memorial," "Everything I Don't Know," "A Certain Dickens," "The Gypsy Road," "Village Landscape"
Seneca Review: "I Was Dreamt," "My Unsurvivor," "Ante-Bird—Scarecrow," "Slowness," "The Empty Places After," "The Jews Left"
Tupelo Quarterly Review: "Papusza," "Life"

"My Attempted Travels" (July 13, 2017) and "Pantarheia" (November 16, 2020) were reprinted in *Poetry Daily*.

"Prayer for the Holy Louse" was reprinted in *The Orison Anthology*, volume 2, 2017.

The text of *Everything I Don't Know* is set in Garamond Premier Pro. Cover photograph of the author by Piotr Wójcik. Cover design by Kyle G. Hunter. Book design by Dakota Jackson.